I0449397

The Circumstances Leading To The Underdevelopment Of Liberia After More Than One Hundred Sixty Years Of Independence

THE CIRCUMSTANCES LEADING TO THE UNDERDEVELOPMENT OF LIBERIA AFTER MORE THAN ONE HUNDRED SIXTY YEARS OF INDEPENDENCE

Samuel K. Ngaima Sr.

Copyright © 2016 by Samuel K. Ngaima Sr.

Library of Congress Control Number:		2016912004
ISBN:	Hardcover	978-1-5245-2881-2
	Softcover	978-1-5245-2880-5
	eBook	978-1-5245-2879-9

All rights reserved. No part of this book may be reproduced or transmitted
in any form or by any means, electronic or mechanical, including photocopying,
recording, or by any information storage and retrieval system,
without permission in writing from the copyright owner.

Any people depicted in stock imagery provided by Thinkstock are models,
and such images are being used for illustrative purposes only.
Certain stock imagery © Thinkstock.

Print information available on the last page.

Rev. date: 08/25/2016

To order additional copies of this book, contact:
Xlibris
Bloomington, IN, 47403, USA
1-888-795-4274
www.Xlibris.com
Orders@Xlibris.com
746996

DEDICATION

This book is dedicated in loving memory of my late parents, Honorable John Ngaima and Madam Korpo Finda Ngaima as a mark of recognition of their sacrificial and invaluable services and love for me and my children. No befitting and sympathetic history can be written about my life without allusion to their investments and imaginations for my future success. Their love, care and affections to me and my children will forever be remembered.

It is with sorrow that I dedicate this book to my parents, as I think about the bullets in the Liberian National conflict that took away both of my parents in 2001, for their only crimes was because they were members of the Gbandi tribe in Kolahun District, Lofa County, Liberia.

Regrettably, President, Charles Taylor's fighters, NPFL refused to release the remains of my father to the family for proper burial. His remains were thrown into a mass grave on Foyia-Kolahun Highway. My parents did not have the heroic funerals that they deserved from their children, grandchildren, great grandchildren and relatives.

Mama and Pa, without your generous contributions and sacrifices to my life, I would not have fulfilled my dreams. Therefore, once again I say "THANK YOU".

FOREWORD

The author of this book analyzes the causes responsible for the underdevelopment of Liberia as the continuous dominations of political, social and economic activities of the Liberian Government for more than 160 years after independence.

The book reveals as one of the underlying reasons for the underdevelopment of Liberia as the marginalization of the indigenous Liberian, the perpetuation of Americo-Liberians' hegemony for more than a century. The rampant corruption and disparities in the political, educational, medical and economic opportunities among the Liberian citizens were all major causes of lack of development since independence in 1847. The findings in the book exposed social stratifications and exclusions of the indigenous Liberians from the political and economic activities as well as the perpetuation of oligarchic regimes of the Americo-Liberians were identified as prime causes for the underdevelopment of Liberia.

The author advocates that Liberia needs a new society with policies of inclusions and equal opportunities that should be implemented to promote sustainable development and reduce poverty among the citizens. In addition, the author advances that the international communities should provide logistical and financial support for building the country and creating the condition for lasting peace, unity and stability. He suggested a new society that must develops policies for equal opportunities for all Liberians regardless of the political, social and economic status.

PREFACE

Dr. Samuel K. Ngaima, Sr. believed that Liberians and other stakeholders need to know the reasons for the lack of development and the magnitude of poverty in Liberia. Therefore, he analyzes the political, historical, social, cultural and economic reasons as well as identifies organizations, groups and individuals responsible for the lack of development in Africa's oldest republic; such factors as marginalization and social stratification instituted by the Americo-Liberians against the indigenous people, perpetuation of the their oligarchic regime for more than one hundred fifty years after independence in 1847. The exclusions of the majority-indigenous Liberians from the political and economic activities of their country were prime causes for the lack of development of the nation. The author discusses the factors responsible for the destructions of most of the infrastructures of the nation.

The findings found in this book revealed that perpetuation of Americo-Liberians hegemony on political powers and their methods of governance as well the resulting disparities in political, educational, medical, economic and social opportunities were major causes of Liberia's underdevelopment and magnitude of poverty. The author also pointed out that the unique formation of the Country and subsequent leadership style and the social stratification for more than 150 years of Americo-Liberian oligarchic regime was considered as one of the causes of lack of development. Dr. Ngaima is convinced that this book is relevant in today's society because the information will provide awareness and education tor the Liberian people and other investors in the Country so as to avoid the mistakes of the past. He further believed that his book promotes equality, justice, and egalitarian which are crucial values for the promotion of peace, social stability and sustainable development in Liberia.

Acknowledgements

I am most grateful to the Almighty God, who blessed me to survive the bloody Liberian civil conflicts, the outbreak of Ebola virus in Liberia and all the evils of society and granted me the opportunities to embark on this project. For without His Grace and Blessing, I may not have been alive like my parents, many of my relatives, friends and professional colleagues who died as a result of the Liberian civil conflicts and the outbreak of Ebola virus.

The accomplishments of writing and publishing this book was only possible with the earlier love, financial supports and care of my late parents, Honorable John Ngaima and Korpo Finda Ngaima. My special thanks and appreciation to my lovely children: Sayba Rose Ngaima-Tarwo, Korpo Finda Ngaima-Hanson, John Ngaima, Korpo Buttuh Ngaima-Nyumah, Sam Kpehe Ngaima, Jr. Abbey Jowo Ngaima, Momo Ngaima, Joseph Ngaima, Sanuel K. Ngaima, Jr. and Kafalyn Korpo (KK) Ngaima, as well as my nephew Albert Sangbeh Jallah I give special commitments in the memory of my dear son, the late Martin Samuel Ngaima, who was taken away from us by the bullets of arm-robbers in Detroit, Michigan, USA. The love and support of my children have been a great blessing, motivation and encouragement as they brightened my life achievements.

I am extraordinarily grateful to my caring and lovely grandchildren: Prince Ngaima, Abraham Ngaima, Vajohlyne Miatta Pajibo, Presko Hanson, Felicia Philips, Sonnette Nyemah, Daydor Philips, Jr. Martina Ngaima, Jartu Ngaima, Martin Samuel Ngaima, Jr., Presilyn Hanson,

Amy Nyemah, Praise Hanson, Fatima Wilson, Deborah Ngaima, Tristan Samuel Ngaima, Alaric Wilson, Mathew Ngaima, John Ngaima, Jr. and Fayia Johnson for the opportunities granted me to complete this book without feeling guilty because of the time that we missed together. My special love and gratitude to madam, Winde Akoi whose ideas helped me to complete this book.

My special gratitude to my brothers, sisters, cousins, nephews and nieces as well as other relatives in Liberia and united States of America and other parts of the World. I am dearly grateful to my sons in-law and daughters in-law for their inspirations given to me during the period of writing this book. I am also grateful to my children's mothers for their cooperation. I am very thankful to Dr. Abeodu Jones and Dr. Nyemah Jones for their moral supports, my friend J. Ninsel Warner for helping to proof read and my thanks to my friend, Uncle,-Raphael M. Kpissay for his encouragement, my nephew, Rev. G. Laurenzo Stevens, and his wife, Rebecca Stevens as well as the man I refer to as my friend and brother, James S. Worlobah and his wife, Marilyn Worlobah, my cousin, Joseph M. Seley and all the seley family in Liberia and the United States of America. Finally, many thanks to all the employees of Liberia Acquatic Solution for the hard work and cooperation.

CONTENTS

CHAPTER ONE

WHY IS LIBERIA UNDERDEVELOPED AFTER ONE HUNDRED SIXTY (160) YEARS OF INDEPENDENCE?

Introduction

The purpose of this book is not to change the Liberian history but to correct the events that have taken place, which led to the underdevelopment of our common Country-Liberia. It finds a lasting solution to our problems, as well as to end the disunity caused by the Settlers since establishing Liberia in 1822. In short, the author has no intentions to alter what has already taken place but has the desire to let the readers know some of the reasons that led to the lack of development of the first West African republic.

There are many causes, organizations, and individuals responsible for the underdevelopment and level of poverty in Liberia. Several authors identified causes that were responsible for the lack of development such authors as S. Augustu P. Horton in 1996, Professor, Rufus N. Darkortey in 2007, Philip Tali, Jr. in 2012, Abraham M. Keita in 2015 and other non-Liberian scholars includes Professor, Joseph Stiglize in 2004, Dr. Erithj Kuhnen in 1992, as well as Sachs and Warne (2001), Stevens (2003), Homewood (1962), New-Havens (1964) and Tubingen (1992), among others. Although, these authors, scholars and publishers have discussed dozens of causes and people who are responsible for the underdevelopment of Liberia, none has identified the prime reasons for the lack of development in Africa's first independent republic for more than three decades as this book tries to do. Based on these publications, concerns and other theoretical explanations this book tries to introduce to the readers the core reasons for the underdevelopment of Liberia without aiming at completeness. There are different theories, which are the basis for our analysis and discussions. These theories help to differentiate between various observations and facts. Others differentiate between socialistic and market-economy oriented theories because these two groups have different ways of analyzing and diagnosing the causes of underdevelopment. They are distinct as to their opinion on the possibilities of reform or revolution with a view of influencing the development process.

During the early days after independence, development efforts were not given priorities, thus the lack of loads, bridges, buildings and human improvements. Since the end of World War II, Liberians have experienced struggles for the improvement of their living conditions in the first African republic. At the beginning, there was little question as to the causes of underdevelopment; the newly independent countries as well as United Nations bodies and industrialized countries tried to promote development by applying measures like the introduction of know-how through the assignment of experts, the expansions of education, the development of infrastructure.

In the case of Liberia, just as the Economic Watch (2012) indicated, it became obvious that this was more or less a treatment of symptoms instead of causes, and the gap gradually widened between the developed and less developed countries of this world. Theoretical considerations at this time were explained from the viewpoint of western nations. The viewpoints of developing countries gained momentum in development theory which offers justification for policies. Different positions in development policy are based on the variations in underlying development theories.

This book has uncovered several factors that led to the underdevelopment of Liberia and the impacts on the historical, political, religious, social, and cultural improvement of the Country. It has also determined the extent to which these factors have contributed to the destructions in the country.

Furthermore, in current day Liberia, the family, clan, and ethnic groups are still the essential bedrocks for social and political enlargement in the Country. Nevertheless, in order to improve on the political growth and expansion coming from alliances of our Liberian leaders, we must formulate a new concept of the common good based on ethnic identities and political consensus. Ethnic identities should be tolerated on the basis of the common good.

Moreover, since the many years of independence, it is about time that Liberians heal the scars created by the mistakes of our past leaders resulting in the lack of physical and psychological development. The Country should move forward by creating a new society in which all Liberians will be treated equally before the law. As a believer in history, I feel that in order to promote development, we must correct the wrongs that led to lack of development. The true stories must be told for the necessary corrections to be made and to avoid similar wrongs in the future. Liberians should be honest to each other with the view of correcting the past for a brighter future. The Liberian political system is dysfunctional with no plan in place to help resolve the problems of underdevelopment and inequalities.

Chapter Two

The Establishment of Africa's First Independent Republic: Liberia

In order for our readers to fully understand and appreciate the rationale for discussing the causes to the lack of development, we wish to further discuss the problems created by the establishment of Liberia and the leadership style that followed. The discussions about the founding and events leading to the establishment and premature independence of Liberia, as African's first independent republic need to be explained. What made Liberia as being unique in the history of Africa should be fully explained?

2.1 Events preceding the Founding of Liberia

The scholarly consensus is that the establishment of Liberia in 1822 by a philanthropic organization, the American Colonization Society (ACS), and the leadership structures that were put in place, led to political confrontations and the underdevelopment of Liberia. Ironically, this situation was an outcome of the same tensions and contradictions that existed in the United States between black slaves and their white masters.

President, Abraham Lincoln's Emancipation Proclamation outlawed slavery in the Confederate territory of the United States and created the foundations to eventually abolish slavery everywhere in the country. This declaration unintentionally divided the Americans society between the antislavery activists and the abolitionists. The antislavery activists wanted to establish the American Colonization Society (ACS) to remove both the freed black slaves and enslaved African Americans from the American society. They tried to resolve the deliberations over slavery in the United States. The diverse groups of antislavery activists were credited for establishing the ACS in 1817. The goals of the organization were to remove both free black slaves and enslaved African Americans from the United States and send them back to Africa. They felt that a biracial (two races) society was not possible in the United States of America. Therefore, forcibly returning the freed slaves and enslaved African Americans to their original home in Africa was the only way to bring an end to racial conflict in America.

On the other hand, the abolitionists, mainly radical Republicans and some African American leaders like Frederick Douglass, strongly believed that it was wrong to free the slaves only to return them to Africa. They considered this as an outrageous injustice. Other leading African Americans saw abolition of slavery as the first step in establishing racial equality in the United States, and that when the white people and freed blacks lived in close proximity to one another, it could foster racial harmony and prevent a major segregation. Although the organizers of the ACS presented themselves as humanitarians and opposed the evils of slavery, many white advocates of colonization objected to the presence of free blacks in American society.

Many white Americans felt that African Americans, who were slaves to white masters could not be economically successful living in the white American society as free people. Some white people considered the freed blacks as physically and mentally inferior to white people. There were others who believed that the racism and societal separation resulting from slavery were major obstacles for integration of the black race. Thomas Jefferson was one of those who suggested relocating free blacks outside the United States to settle in Africa. Meanwhile, the number of free African Americans (people of color) was increasing each year.

In 1822 the ACS established the colony of Liberia. It assisted thousands of former African-American slaves and free blacks (with legislated limits) to emigrate from the United States to Africa-Liberia. Many white people saw this as preferable to emancipation in the United States. Henry Clay, one of the founders of the ACS said that blacks faced unconquerable prejudice resulting from their colors as being Black: they never could amalgamate with the free whites of this country. It was desirable, therefore, to remove them from the shores of the white man.

In an effort to resolve the debate over slavery in the United States, a diverse group of antislavery activists are credited for establishing the American Colonization Society (ACS) in 1817. The organization's goal was to remove both free and enslaved African Americans from the United States and transport them to Africa. The members of the ACS believed biracial society was not possible in the United States and therefore, forcibly returning the African Americans to Africa was the only solution that could bring an end to racial conflict in America. The extreme nature of their good intentions undermined the society's popular petitions and brought them into direct conflict with antislavery groups, particularly abolitionists, Radical Republicans, and African American leaders, such as Frederick Douglass.

The supporters of colonization believed that racial conflict was inevitable, when white and black Americans lived in close proximity to one another, and thus they turned to colonization as a solution to America's race problem. Although colonization supporters presented themselves as humanitarian evils, many white advocates of colonization objected to the presence of free blacks in American society. The supporters of African colonization also believed that it would both preserve racial harmony and avert a major sectional crisis. On the hand, abolitionists believed strongly in the possibility of a biracial society and adamantly rejected the notion that racial conflict could end only if African Americans left the United States. For example, Frederick Douglass and other leading African Americans saw abolition as the first step in establishing racial equality in the United States but the idea of freeing the slaves only to remove them to Africa struck Douglass and his compatriots as an outrageous injustice.

Many white citizens of the American society thought that African Americans could not succeed in living in their society as free people. Some considered blacks physically and mentally inferior to whites, and others believed that the racism and societal polarization resulting from slavery were insurmountable obstacles for integration of the black races. Thomas Jefferson was among those who proposed relocating free blacks outside the United States to settle in Africa. Meanwhile, efforts to secure United States Federal support were rebuffed and the triumph of democracy blocked the support necessary for a successful program. The number of free African American (people of color) increased yearly; in 1790, there were 59,467 free blacks, out of a total U.S. population of almost four (4) million. By 1800, there were 108,378 free blacks in a population of 7.2 million. These factors significantly influenced the popularity of the organization of the American Colonization Society (ACS) as a solution to the "problems" of free blacks. As Richardson (1959) indicted, the first ship, *Mayflower of Liberia* (formerly *Elizabeth*), departed New York on February 6, 1820, for West Africa, with 86 settlers.

2.2 The Establishment of Liberia as Sanctuary for freed American Slaves

Between 1821 and 1838, the American Colonization Society established the first settlement, which is now known as Liberia. The colonists of African-American descents became known as Americo-Liberians. They considered themselves first as American citizens before their Liberian citizenship. Not only were many of them racially mixed and western descents, their education, religion and culture made them different from the indigenous people who were found on the land with whom they did not identify.

The slaveholders argued that it would be better for blacks to settle in Africa. Slave owners opposed freedom for blacks, but saw repatriation as a way of avoiding rebellions. Therefore, repatriation of Black Americans to Africa was not only done on humanities for the interest of the Blacks but the interests and safety of the white Americans.

Liberia shared a similar history with Sierra Leone in that the two West African neighbors owed their contemporary existence to the emergence of philanthropic organizations in Europe and the United States that were eager to find a permanent asylum in Africa for their free blacks. The American and European politicians felt that the "freed men of color," as they were called, had become a serious social and economic burden on the white-dominated societies of Europe and the United States.

Economically, Liberia was founded with the help and financial contributions of some citizens of the United States and the government of America through the ACS. The country, Liberia, is one of two African states in the world that was established by the western World as a home for former slaves and their descendants. The other country is Sierra Leone, which also began as a place for resettlement of band poor blacks from Britain.

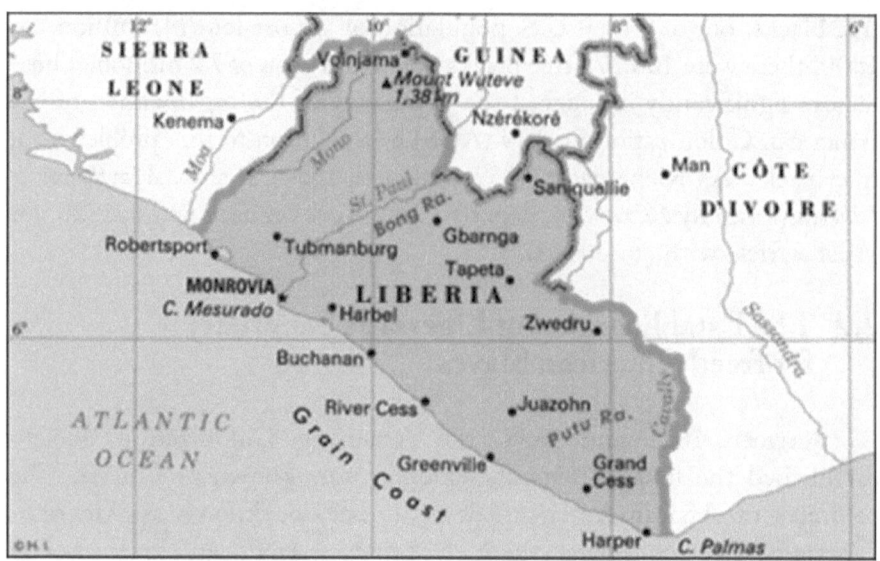

Liberia was faced with border problems originating from the French and the British. By 1909, the British took a portion of Liberia's land and annexed it to Sierra Leone in an area now in the borderlands near Bo in Sierra Leone. The French also annexed large sections of Liberian territory around the Cavalla River in Ivory Coast and the area now known as Kissidu in Guinea. Liberia had no military power to stop these annexations or to reclaim these lands taken by the two Western powers. Therefore, the Country accepted to become independent while they were not prepared.

Liberia is unique in Africa; it is the oldest independent black republic in Africa. The country lies a few degrees north of the equator. Current-day Liberia covers approximately 43,000 square miles, about the size of the state of Tennessee, because several parts of the original country were taken away by the French and the British. The strip of coastline of Liberia extends 370 miles alongside the Atlantic Ocean between Sierra Leone on the northwest and the Ivory Coast on the southeast. Republic of Guinea borders Liberia on the north.

The average population density in Liberia is about forty-nine people per square mile, and more than 66 percent of the population resides in the rural part of the country. As indicated in the 2008 Liberian national census report, the population of Liberia is 3,476,608 people of which 1,118,241 people lived in Montserrado County, the most populous county in the country. An estimated 970,824 people live in Monrovia, the capital city.

Further, the 2008 census report in the revealed that Monrovia is four times more populous than all the 14 county capitals combined.

The result of the 2008 national census also showed that 85.5 percent of the population practices Christianity. Muslims comprise 12.2 percent of the population, largely coming from the Mandingo and Vai as well as other ethnic groups. Liberian Muslims are divided into Sunnis, Shias, Ahmadiyyas, Sufis, and nondenominational Muslims.

Traditional indigenous religions are practiced by 0.5 percent of the population, while 1.5 percent subscribe to no religion. A very small number of people practice Bahá'í, Hindu, Sikh, or Buddhist beliefs. Christianity is concurrent participation with indigenous religious societies such as Poro and Sande is common in Liberia.

The educational survey conducted by the UNESCO (2010) showed that the literacy rate of Liberia was estimated at 60.8 percent (64.8 percent for males and 56.8 percent for females). In some places in the country, primary and secondary education is free, but in other areas, children are required to pay tuition or some fees to attend school. The country's educational sector is hampered by inadequate schools and supplies, as well as a lack of qualified teachers. Higher education is provided by a number of public and private universities.

The University of Liberia first opened its doors in 1862 as the country's largest and oldest university. Currently, the University of Liberia has six colleges, a master degree school with four programs, a medical school and the nation's only law school, Louis Arthur Grimes School of Law. In 2009, Tubman University in Harper, Maryland County, became the second public university in Liberia. Cuttington University, established by the Episcopal Church of the USA in 1889 in Suakoko, Bong County, is the nation's oldest private university. Since 2006, the government has also opened community colleges in Buchanan, Gbanga, Sengai, Sanniquellie, and Voinjama.

As found in the World Health Organization (2010) report, the civil friction which ended in 2003 destroyed about 95 percent of Liberia's health facilities and left Liberian hospitals in poor conditions, sorely lacking in maintenance, equipment, and staff. Life expectancy in Liberia is estimated to be 57.4 years. The WHO (2010) report indicated that a number of highly communicable diseases are easily spread in Liberia, including HIV, tuberculosis, malaria, and diarrheal diseases. In June 2014, an outbreak of Ebola virus from Guinea spread to Liberia. By November 4, 2014, the government as Liberia confirmed the death toll of 2,766 and 6,619 people who were affected by the disease.

These death toll and people affected by the epidemic were double those of both of the two neighboring countries (Sierra Leone, 1,130 deaths, and Guinea, 1,054). In August 2014, Guinea, a country where the outbreak began, closed its borders to Liberia to help contain the spread of the virus, as more new cases were being reported in Liberia than in Guinea. On August 16, 2014, a quarantine center in Monrovia was attacked by protesters, causing a number of patients being monitored for Ebola to flee, while blood-soaked beddings and other infected items were looted by angry protesters. The incident was seen by the international community as a disaster and it had the potential to accelerate the spread of the disease.

The Liberian history as an independent nation began with the arrival of the freed black Americans. The black Americans who settled in this part of the world referred to themselves as Americo-Liberians. As indicated earlier, Liberia was established under the auspices of the American colonization in 1822 as a sanctuary for freed black slaves. On July 26, 1847, Liberia hastily became an independent nation through the directives of the board of directors of the ACS.

As Sirleaf (2003) mentioned, the Liberian government recognized seventeen (17) ethnic groups. The Americo-Liberians or the repatriated free black slaves, add to the sixteen indigenous ethnic groups to make up the seventeenth ethnic group of Liberia. The original ethnic groups include Bassa, Belle, Dey, Gbandi (of which the author is a member), Gio, Gola, Grebo, Kpelle, Kissi, Krahn, Kru Lorma, Mandingo, Mano, Mendi Sapo and Vai. The traditional education and cultural format of the natives (the tribes) were not only unacceptable but were also condemned by the settlers and referred to them as devils.

The difference between Liberia and most countries in Africa and Europe are fundamental in nature, as many scholars agreed that Liberia has never being subjected to colonial rule and has never experienced the anti-elitist movement by driving out foreign colonizers and casting out white culture. Liberian leaders have pursued to preserve their historical and political system rather than abandon it. However, as I indicated earlier, Liberia was founded under the auspices of the ACS, sponsored by contributions from missionaries and charitable organizations as well as individual Americans.

The motives for these supports range from missionary desires for bringing Christianity to Africa to the wishes of the Southerners to get rid of free Black slaves, who they considered as second-class citizens, from the American society. The ACS also sought the supports and blessing of the government of the United States. For example, Sirleaf (2003) acknowledged that the United States Congress and President, James Monroe provided a grant of $100,000 to the ACS for the purpose of establishing Liberia, getting the blacks out of America and resettlement of repatriates from the United States.

On July 26, 1847, when the commonwealth proclaimed its independence, the settlers were made of only three thousand men as the indigenous people, and women were not part of the Liberian Government. The Liberian constitution was drawn up along the same lines of the United States. A presidential election was held for the first time in the newly independent country on October 5, 1847. Although, Gov. Joseph Jenkins Roberts of the pro-administration party was out of the city at the time of the elections, he was declared the winner, thereby defeating Samuel Benedict of the anti-administration party. Governor Roberts was inaugurated as the first president of Liberia on January 3, 1848, with Nathaniel Brander as his vice president, without opportunities for challenges.

President Joseph Jenkins Roberts
First President of Liberia

2.3 Social Change and the Economy Deprivation in Liberia

The Americo-Liberians created their own social order in Liberia and dominated every aspect of the Liberian society. Even though they were originally Africans, Americo-Liberians practice American lifestyle, cultural and social values. They, like many westerners, believed in the religious superiority of Christianity and the American and European cultural superiority over indigenous African cultures. They created social structures based on American way of life and maintained Western ways of speaking English. The Americo-Liberians imposed English as the official language for governmental business, formal education, and the mass media. In addition, the Americo-Liberians were building churches and houses that resembled those of the people from southern United States.

They named places after American people and states, such as Monrovia after President Monroe, the city of Virginia after the state of Virginia, Maryland County after the state of Maryland in America among many other names. Although, the Americo-Liberians were only 5 percent of the population of Liberia, they controlled all the major resources which helped them to dominate the native peoples. They had access to the ocean, tax revenues, modern technical skills, literacy and higher levels of education as well as valuable relationships with many American institutions, like the government of America and the Free-masonry.

After World War II, many indigenous Liberians came to the coastal regions in search of jobs and Western education. The Americo-Liberian government had earlier opposed this type of migration, but it was too late to stop it. When President Tubman became president of Liberia, these social tensions made him to grant franchise to the indigenous Liberians in 1951 and to enfranchise the women. The continuous economic disparities that existed between Americo-Liberian and the native (indigenous) Liberians created hostility between them. President Tubman used these opportunities to repress political opposition and to rig elections because he felt that the natives were in his favor.

The Liberian economy was dependent mainly on agricultural products for export. Liberia's coffee industry was destroyed in the 1870s by the competition of coffee from Brazil. In addition, European technology drove Liberian shipping companies out of business. The Liberian national currency collapsed in 1907, and the country was forced to adopt the U.S. dollar.

In 1926, Liberia granted a concession agreement to an American rubber company, Firestone, at Harbel, Liberia. This industry created more than twenty-five thousand jobs and soon became the backbone of the Liberian economy. In 1927, Liberia was accused of forcibly recruiting and selling indigenous people as contract laborers which was considered as slavery. The investigative report of the League of Nations reprimanded Liberia for practicing and fostering forced labor as well as gross intimidation and suppression of the native. President King and his vice president were forced to resign. Between 1947 and 1960, exports of iron, timber, and rubber strongly supported the Liberian economy. For example, prior to 1971, Liberia had the world's largest rubber industry and the largest ship registrations in the world.

2.4 Rebellions and Confrontations in the Republic of Liberia

A series of rebellions within the indigenous Liberian population took place between the 1850s and 1920s. For example in 1854, the settlers from the State of Maryland refused to join the colony in Monrovia and declared their own nationhood. The newly proclaimed African-American country in the region: Maryland in Africa, was forced by an insurgency of the Grebo and the Kru people to join Liberia. This rebellion was instrumented by the Americo-Liberian Government. Liberia's expansion brought the colony into border disputes with the French and British colonists in French -Guinea and Ivory Coast and the British -Sierra Leone. The presence and protection of the United States Navy in West Africa, until 1916, prevented military threats to Liberian territory and independence.

The Liberian Constitution as Nelson (1984) stated provided for freedom of religion, and the government generally respects this right. While separation of church and state is also mandated by the Constitution. Liberians are mainly considered as Christians in practice. Public schools offer biblical studies, though parents may get their children. Commerce is prohibited by law on Sunday and authorities were mandated to excuse Muslim students for Friday prayers.

The 2008 National Census also showed that 85.5% of the population practices Christianity. Muslims comprise 12.2% of the population, largely coming from the Mandingo and Vai as well as other ethnic groups. Liberian Muslims are divided into Sunnis, Shias, Ahmadiyyas, Sufis, and non-denominational Muslims. Traditional indigenous religions are practiced by 0.5% of the population, while 1.5% subscribe to no religion. A very small number of people are Baha'is, Hindu, Sikh, or Buddhist. Concurrent participation in indigenous religious secret societies such as Poro and Sande is common.

2.5 Separation of the Liberians into Two Layers of Citizens

A series of rebellions among the indigenous Liberian population took place between the 1850s and 1920s. For example in 1854, as indicated else where the settlement in Maryland refused to join the colony in Monrovia and declared their own nationhood. The newly African-American nation in the region, the state of Maryland was forced by an insurgency of the Grebo and the Kru people to join Liberia. Although, the Africans were not accepted as part of the Liberian Government, their actions against Maryland were instrumented by the Settlers in Monrovia. Liberia's expansion brought the colony into border disputes with the French and British colonists in French -Guinea and Ivory Coast and the British -Sierra Leone. The presence and protection of the United States Navy in West Africa, until 1916, prevented military threats to Liberian territory and independence.

The traditional education and cultural format of the natives were not only unacceptable but was condemned by the Settlers and they referred to African cultures as devils. I have understood from historical events and other experiences that when the majority of the citizens are suppressed and imposed upon, they will usually revolt against their oppressors. In the case of Liberia, the ethnic groups or indigenous Africans opposed the Americo-Liberians' dominations and discriminations.

As Sawyer (1992) stressed, the African majority in Liberia came to perceive the Americo-Liberians to be no better than the European colonizers. Many indigenous Liberians felt that if the Europeans must give up control in Africa, Liberia's own oppressors — the settlers – must do likewise. This notion, was the beginning of internal ethnic conflict in Liberia.

The growing economic and social disparities between Americo-Liberians and the native (Indigenous) Liberians increased hostility between indigenous groups and Americo-Liberians and stalled development in the county. These social tensions led President Tubman to enfranchise the indigenous Liberians men in 1951 and the women in 1963. These enfranchisements made Tubman continued to repress political opposition and to rig elections.

The social order in Liberia was dominated by Americo-Liberians. Although they were African origins, Americo-Liberians held American-life style, cultural and social values. Like many Americans and Europeans, the Americo-Liberians believed that Christianity is superior to other religions and that European civilization is also superior to those of African Animalism and culture.

The Americo-Liberians created communities and social infrastructure closely based on American society, maintaining their English-speaking styles, Americanized way of life, and building churches and houses resembling those of the southern United States of America. Although, they were never more than five percent of the population of Liberia, Americo-Liberians controlled key resources that allowed them to dominate the local or native peoples: access to the ocean, national resources, modern technical skills, literacy and higher levels of education, and valuable relationships with many American institutions, including the American government as well as the Free masonry.

Based on the system of racial segregation in America, the Americo-Liberians recreated a cultural and social caste system with themselves at the top and indigenous Liberians at the bottom. They did not believe in a form of equality with the natives. They felt that natives had the potential to become "civilized" only through conversion to Christianity and western education.

In addition, the Americo-Liberian rule was characterized by brutality, corruptions, exploitations, human rights abuses, and mismanagement of public resources. For example indigenous men were deployed in the army -- formerly the Liberian Frontier Force — to forcibly collect hut taxes from their African brothers for a government in which they were not represented or allowed to participate. The year 1964 was the first time the in the history of Liberia that the hinterland people were represented in the national legislature of Liberia. Prior to this time, indigenous Liberians even interested in observing proceedings of the National Legislature of Liberia were required to deposit with the government in Monrovia the amount of one hundred United States dollars ($100.00). This assertion was confirmed by Umoden (1998) that "the tribal people had been taxed to support a government in which they were never represented" (p. 9). Another example was that in the hinterland, the indigenous people were forcibly recruited to perform government public works to build and maintain public roads as well as to work on the plantations of some Americo-Liberians without pay. This was another form of slavery practiced by descendants of former American slaves.

Sawyer (1996) observed that even the motto inscribed on Liberia's official coat of arms, "*The Love of Liberty Brought Us Here*", excluded the Africans who were living on the land before the settlers arrived. Such exclusions extended to the Africans from government employment and taxation without representation which greatly contributed to the military coup and the level of violence in Liberia. Feeling excluded from their government, the Africans began to identify themselves with individual ethnic groups instead of looking at themselves as Liberians. This separation from the African majority became a factor in the underdevelopment of Liberia.

CHAPTER THREE

HOW WAS LIBERIA, THE FIRST AFRICAN REPUBLIC GOVERNED?

From 1822 to 1847, American agents, both whites and blacks governed Liberia on behalf of the Colonization Society. The most outstanding of these agents was Jehudi Ashman, who ruled Liberia from 1822 until his death in 1828. Other agents included Eli Ayres, Richard Randall, Joseph Michelin, George R. McGill, John B. Pinney, Nathaniel Brander, Ezekiel Skinner, and Anthony D. Williams. Thomas Buchanan and Joseph Jenkins Roberts were the only two governors when the settlement became a Commonwealth of Liberia.

3.1 Political Oppressions and Domination

Thomas Buchanan, the first governor of the Commonwealth of Liberia, was a white American but his successor, Joseph Jenkins Robert was a mulatto-American who became the first President of the Republic of Liberia while William Richard Tolbert, Jr. was the last successive Americo-Liberian presidents before the civil war. The presidential leadership from 1848 to 2003 was limited to Americo-Liberians—both mulattos and dark-skinned settlers—with the exception of one indigenous Liberian, Samuel K. Doe. Thirteen of these presidents were actually born in the United States, so considered themselves first as American citizens and their Liberian citizenship was second.

Politically, Liberia was mostly dominated by two political parties. This means that generally, the Country was governed by two political parties: The Liberian Party (later the Republican Party), was supported primarily by mulattos from poorer backgrounds, while the True Whig Party received much of its following from richer blacks or dark skin Americo-Liberians. The franchise was deliberately limited to Americo-Liberian men and prevented indigenous Liberians and women from voting in elections. From the first presidential election in 1847, the Liberian Party held political dominance and used its position of power to attempt to cripple its opposition. However, in 1869, the True Whigs Party won the presidential election under leadership of Edward James Roye. Although Roye was deposed after just two years of taking office by the Liberian Party dominated Legislature, and the Liberian Party returned to government. However, the True Whigs Party regained power in 1878 and held power constantly afterwards until 1980.

The Liberian Constitution provides that executive power in Liberia is exercised by the president and legislative power is carried out by a two-chamber house of the legislature while the judicial powers are exercised by the Supreme Court and lower courts. The longest-serving president in Liberian history was William V. S. Tubman, who served from 1944 until his death in 1971, while James Skivring Smith served the shortest term in the history of Liberia, serving for two months.

Liberia was originally founded as a place of asylum for American freed black slaves and their descendants -the tiny elite of about 300 extended families, especially during the Tubman and Tolbert administrations. They ruled the country for over a hundred thirty-three (133) years, exhibiting a sense of superiority and exercising dominance over the indigenous Africans, who saw themselves as being exploited by their fellow blacks. The political, social, and economic life of Liberia from 1822 to 1980 was controlled by few citizens- Americo-Liberian families- whose reign was interrupted only briefly from 1980 to 1989 by a military coup.

The Americo-Liberians developed several policies designed to prevent any challenge to their leadership and any political violence. The methods of governance that were introduced by the settlers more than a century ago deteriorated into political oppressions and led to preferential treatments in administering the affairs of the Liberian government.

Subsequently, President, William Vacanarat Shadrach Tubman is best known for his policies of National Unification and the economic Open

Door. He tried to reconcile the interests of the native tribes with those of the Americo-Liberian elite, and increased foreign investments in Liberia to stimulate economic growth. As a result, by 1950s, Liberia had the second-highest rate of economic growth in the world. By the time of his death in 1971 in a London clinic, Liberia had the largest mercantile fleet of ships in the world, the world's largest rubber industry, was the third-largest exporter of iron ore in the world, and had attracted more than US$1 billion in foreign investment

After a gunman attempted to assassinate Tubman in 1955, he brutally repressed the political oppositions. His administration was increasingly authoritarian. The nation's constitution did not have term limits, and Tubman did not volunteer to leave office. He controlled the political party and created a wide network of obligations through patronage systems. He appointed people not based on qualifications but based on patronage.

President, William R. Tolbert
He was assassinated in a Military Coup On April 12, 1980

Yet, another clear example of corruption and the mismanagement of the Country's resources during the Americo-Liberian rule, was seen at the time when the Liberian government was facing a serious financial crisis, President, William Richard Tolbert spent nearly $20 million on the huge and prestigious Hotel Africa and the Organization of Africa Unity (OAU) complex. The land on which the hotel and the complex were located was purchased from the Tolbert family, who dictated not only the price of their land but the method of payment as well the cost of the OAU project. The huge investment brought little or no return to the country once the OAU meetings was over. Today most of the buildings are crumbling by erosion from the Atlantic Ocean and no funds are available to rehabilitate them.

President Tolbert's administration was another clear example of the nepotism and corruption in Liberia. During President Tolbert's administration and before 1980. Minister of Finance Steve Tolbert was the president's younger brother, President Pro-Tempore of the Liberian Senate, Frank E. Tolbert was his older brother, Speaker of the Liberian House of Representatives, Richard A. Henries was his first cousin, and the city mayor for the seat of government for the Montserrado County was his older sister, Lucia Tolbert.

In addition, the president's first son, Adolphus Benedict Tolbert, was selected as a member of the House of Representatives and chairman of the powerful Executive Committee, and the president's two daughters, Christine Tolbert-Norman and Charlotte Tolbert-Tucker, were deputy ministers of education, one in charge of instruction and the other for supervision. The President appointed his third daughter, Wilhelmina Tolbert- Holder, as Liberia's representative to WHO. The president's two sons-in-laws were in charge of the prestigious ministries of Public Works and Education, while the president's nephew Wessiah McClain was the Minister of Commence, Industry, and Transportation. The President's other family members and relatives were appointed in various prestigious positions in Government. What opportunities for employment in Government did the indigenous Liberians and other family members have to get positions in Government?

In the 1980s, a Master Sergeant and 16 enlisted men of the Army deposed President, Tolbert Government and shortly Samuel K. Doe's government increasingly adopted an ethnic outlook as members of his Krahn ethnic group dominated political and military life in Liberia. This caused a heightened level of ethnic tension leading to frequent hostilities between the politically and militarily dominant Krahns and other ethnic groups in the country. Political parties remained banned until 1984. Elections were held on October 15, 1985, in which Doe's National Democratic Party of Liberia (NDPL) was declared winner. The elections were alleged to have been characterized by widespread fraud and rigging. The period after the elections saw increased human rights abuses, corruption, and ethnic tensions. The standard of living, which had been rising in the 1970s, declined drastically. On November 12, 1985, former Army Commanding General Thomas Quiwonkpa invaded Liberia through neighboring Sierra Leone and almost succeeded in toppling the government of Samuel Doe, but the Krahn-dominated Armed Forces of Liberia repelled Quiwonkpa's attack and executed him in Monrovia.

During Doe's administration "the perception of special treatment for the Krahn ethnic group exceeded reality. The Krahn people were disproportionately represented everywhere in government. President Doe's Krahn ethnic group headed five of the sixteen government ministries in the Liberian government, and the governor of the National Bank, numerous deputy ministers, and assistant ministers were Krahn. In addition to the Commander in Chief in the leadership of the Armed Forces of Liberia, Krahn soldiers headed almost all of the important uniformed divisions in the army, including the elite Executive Mansion Guards, military intelligence, and all three mobile infantry battalions. The Chief of Staff of the army was also Krahn.

In President, Doe's Government, there were no restrictions preventing Krahn people from enlisting in the army, while other ethnic groups were not allowed to join the army. Thus, since1980, the Krahn people according to the Lawyers Committee for Human Rights (1986) "members of a tiny fraction of the Liberian community, appear to have emerged with a disproportionate share of the fruit of indigenous rule" (p. 235). These special treatments created a new nation characterized by envy, jealously, deceit, and wanton killings, as well as served as a basis for ethnocentric factors in the Liberian national conflict.

In a short period after CIC Doe became president, resentment began to take root within the ethnic groups of Liberia, especially the resentments between President Doe's Krahn tribe and Gio and Mano people. The report contended that the tensions between the people of Nimba County mainly Gio and Mano, and Doe's Krahn tribes of Grand Gedeh intensified during and after the foiled coup of General Thomas Quiwonkpa, who was a member of the Gio tribe in Nimba County.

3.2 Party Politics in Liberia

Politically, the leadership and governance in Liberia were mostly dominated by two political parties. This means that generally, the

Country was governed by two political parties: The Liberian Party (later the Republican Party), was supported primarily by mulattos from poorer financial backgrounds, while the True Whig Party received much of its following from richer dark skin Americo-Liberian. The franchise was deliberately limited to Americo-Liberian men and prevented indigenous Liberians and women from participation in the affairs of the Liberian Government.

Again from the first presidential election in 1847, the Liberian Party held political dominance and used its position of power to attempt to cripple its opposition. However, in 1869, the True Whigs Party won the presidential election under leadership of Edward James Roye. Although, President Roye was deposed, just after two years of taking office by the Liberian Party dominated Legislature, the Liberian Party returned to government. However, the True Whigs Party regained power in 1878 and held power continuously until 1980.

Between 1980 and 2006, Liberia was governed by a series of military and/or rebel leaders as well as transitional governments. The last military or rebel president was Pres. Charles Taylor, who was asked by the United States to step down and leave the Country in 2003. He was succeeded by a transitional government. The elections to replace the transitional government took place in October and November 2005, which mustered in Ellen Johnson–Sirleaf as the first female elected President of Liberia.

3.3 Other reasons for the Underdevelopment of Liberia

According to Morgan (2010) the dehumanizing effects of slavery impacts the behaviors of the Americo-Liberians. It caused them to practice the same acts of superiority and discrimination they experienced as slaves in America against the indigenous people of Liberia. Painfully, acts of superiority, discrimination and suppressions were also causes of underdevelopment of Liberia, on the West Coast of Africa.

Scholarly journals, books, and online sources reviewed by author analysis reasons for underdevelopment of Liberia. These sources augmented substantially by expert, such as Hlophe (1997), Richardson (1959), Sirleaf (2000), Nelson (1984), Liebenow (1987), Stevens (2003) Professor Joseph Stiglize in 2004 and others were the main source of the data in detailing why Liberia remains under developed since independence for more than 160 years. Similar exposures to western ways of life eventually descended

Americo-Liberians into a colonial culture which revealed how the slavery experiences caused them to become oppressors.

Many indigenous Liberians wanted to be identified as Americo-Liberians, such as Robert Zango change to Robert Azango, Stephen Kollie became Stephen Kollison, Stephen Yeke became Stephen Yekenson while other wanted to remain Indigenous Liberians by changing their names. Such as Rudolph Roberts change his name to Togba Nah Tipoleh, Thomas Smith became Tom Woewi, Joseph Chesson change his identity to Chea Cheapo, Rudolph T. Johnson became Tambakai Jangabai, Khasu Robert became known as Kona Khasu and David Karlor became Kan Carlor among others. These situation of brain washing played roles in the underdevelopment of a society where one group of citizens feel more important than the others.

The Germanic and Nordic tribes settled in the area now known as England, they worked to integrate with the people they met on the land. On the contrary, the settlers from the United States in Liberia did the exact opposite; they distinguished themselves from the natives of the area, who later became known as 'Indigenous Liberians (Country people).

Most Liberian History books reviewed by the author list the major tribes or ethnic groups in Liberia as 16. The 16 tribes make up about 95% of the population while the Americo-Liberians are only about 5% of the population. The Americo-Liberians and the Congo (pronounced Kongor) from the Caribbean and United States immigrants make up the 17th tribe of Liberia, while immigrants from other African countries like Sierra Leone, Ghana, Nigeria, Togo, etc. fall within the African subgroup as foreign tribes.

Some tribes, based on Biblical evidences were named after their leaders. The tribe of Gbandi (Bandi) is a good example, named after their warrior-chief Gbandi- who migrated from the East Africa. He and his tribes men were said to have first settled in the Togo. In recent times, there are Gbandis in Togo and Liberia, except there are changes now in the languages they speak. According to Cultural anthropologists, a tribe is any of a variety of social units; the term usually referred to a unit of social organization that is culturally homogeneous and consists of multiple kinships.

In modern day Liberia, most tribes are organized as unitary political entities, within which people share a common language and culture. For example, Kolahun District is now made up of predominately Gbandi people while Grand Kru County is mainly Krus and Grand Bassa Counties comprised of mainly the Bassa tribes. Some tribes are confined to a limited territory, sometimes a single small island, within which everyone knows everyone else. The multitude of small tribes further contribute to lack of development. For example the Belle Tribe is confirmed to a single territory-Belle District now within Gbapoly County and almost every one knows everyone else but they are not enough to effect development. A tribe may consist of several villages, which may be cross-cut by clans, grade, associations, or secret societies; such poro and Sandi societies, each of which cross-cutting institutions at different times and in different ways as well as may perform economic, political, legal, and religious functions.

There are several causes for the underdevelopment of the Country because of the mistakes made by the founders of the nation, government officers and even some citizens. They failed to prioritize sustainable development of the Republic of Liberia. The intention of writing this book is to help alter the situation and identifying the sacrifices and contributions made by both African-Liberians and Americo-Liberians to the establishment.

Today, many of the legacies and practices continue to be pandemic in Liberia, just as the Europeans colonizers when they came in contact with the Africans. For example, the Christianity approach to the indigenous Africans traditional religion and way of life was very negative. The African was regarded as primitive human-the country man and as a child. The Country man must be fostered and directed through a process of slow and carefully controlled assimilation toward the right religion-Christianity – and a time in the unclear future when the country people would be integrated into the western way of life.

Regard to corruption, Darkortey (2007) stated that Liberia has a long history of government officials diverting public funds and resources into personal use. Moreover, these officials are aided or abetted by unscrupulous businessmen to deny the nation and its citizens with the most needed basic resources for development and provision of social services and infrastructure. These social ills have become systemic and institutionalized in most public and private sector as means of acquiring easy wealth. In short, corruption has been a major factor to why Liberia's failure to developed since 1847. Every one talk about the evils of corruption but nothing is done to stop corruption in the Country.

For examples, President, William R. Tolbert declared war on corruptions but his administration was seriously involved in corruption to the extent that he was assassinated by Samuel K. Doe for corruption. President, Samuel K. Doe, who over threw an elected government and promised the nation to eradicate corruption, put an end to economic dominations and establish more equitable distributions of the nation's wealth. Once the coup was successful in topping the regime and overthrew an elected government for corruption he became rooted in rampant corruption. Doe was brutally murdered for corruption by Prince Johnson's rebels. Again, President, Ellen Johnson-Sirleaf during her first inauguration speech declared to the cheerful and jovial crown that corruption will be her Government's number one enemy. Critics have it that corruption has become her administration's number one friend; as her government officers and other in position of trust entrenched most in corrupt practices and her government is considered the most corrupt in history of Liberia.

Economy watch (2012) indicated that Liberia's lack of basic infrastructural development is chronically exacerbated by continuous policy inconsistencies as the country's development agenda depends on the political platform of a sitting government. These politicians come to power with unhindered authorities that allow them to conveniently decide how the country must be developed, when such development must occur, where such development must occur, and who should implement such development. This policy is a hindrance to structural and sustainable development in Liberia.

As Darkortey (2007) stated, one of the major problems with such a bad policy is that the development agenda of the country is highly discontinuous, meaning that the development agenda, as designed by a sitting government, will cease to exist when that government ceases to exist. The incoming government does not feel compelled to implement a development agenda of the previous government. It is a plan based on the vision of that past government and not the new administration. While most countries have established short and long term national development plans that all governments or presidents of the country must implement when they take power, Liberia is still continuing a very bad policy of leaving the country development agenda with leaders that have not demonstrated the abilities and desires to holistically develop the country. These bad policies could be stopped by a law that establishes a national development plan for Liberia that transcends all presidents.

Additionally, Liberia is one of the least educated countries in Africa and in the world with an illiteracy rate of more than 60 percent. Furthermore, more than 50 percent of all literate Liberians lack college education, while more than 70 percent of Liberians lacks the requisite modern technological and technical training that is driving successful economic growth in other countries. These statistics are positively linked with the consistencies of bad policies and even the lack of policies on the part of successive Liberian governments to build strong schools and universities around the country that provide the requisite amount of education that strengthens the capacities of the Liberian people to function and compete in the global economy.

For example, the policy of Gradualism in Liberia was a selective policy that the America-Liberians extended to only a few of the assimilated Africans, who would enjoy political benefits such as presidential appointments and memberships in the cabinet as well as the diplomatic service of Liberia. As a result of this policy, few Native Liberians were included in the government.

Some of those Africans who benefited from this policy were Momo Massquoi, a Vai who was appointed Consul General to Germany in 1927; Momolu Dukuly, a Mandingo who became Secretary of State in 1932; and Edward Sumo Jones, a Lorma who was appointed Commissioner of Immigration and Naturalization Service in 1965. These special treatments in the Liberian government granted by the ruling elite demonstrated to the African masses that their cooperation with the America-Liberians had advantages.

Another example was President Tubman's Open Door Policy which led to gross exploitations of Country's lands, uneven development, and further extension of America-Liberian powers and dominations in both the public and private sectors. The marginal inclusions of these indigenous Liberians, whom the ruling elite employed as an indigenous *esprit de corps.* The Africans used the experiences to their advantages to eventually unseat the ruling elite in 1980. The 1979 Rice Riot was a precursor to the 1980 military coup followed by the present Liberian conflict.

The National Unification and Integration Policy launched in 1944 by William V.S. Tubman and President Tolbert's policy of "Mat to Mattress" in 1972, all came too late to correct the unbridgeable fragmentation between the African ethnic groups and the America-Liberians. The Liberian ruling elites and their governments had sown the seeds of divisive conflict and violence, all of which contributed to the lack of development. Their policies, prior to the military coup were too late to defuse the tensions.

In their debates with the Americo-Liberians as adversaries, the native accused the Americo-Liberian tribe of monopolizing every conceivable socio-cultural, political and economic activities in Liberia, since the inception of the country. They believed that the land and the resources of the country were misused by these Americo-Liberians, as if they were their personal properties. Many times the educated Indigenous Liberian engaged these Americo-Liberians and their wards in heated but civil debates, without resorting to personal attacks.

For more than one hundred fifty (150) years of attempted co-habitations with the settlers, the Americo-Liberians have shown no willingness to understand the culture that is all around them. The tribes men have made every attempt to let them know who they were but the Americo-Liberians condemned the Africans to the stack of useless verbosity as "tribalism." The Americo-Liberians remained stagnant because they refused the infusions of the values of the cultural majority. The Americo-Liberians feared that African cultures could have influence on their social life and would corrupt their Western profile. Similarly, the Liberian society remained disgustingly underdeveloped with bad imitations of Western culture. The Americo-Liberians demonstrated that the most appropriate means of being civilized was through Christianity, American ways of dressing (three piece and tail coat suits) and speaking English.

When you talk about ramble from period the slaves were taken to America to the time of the migration of freed slaves and their descendants, the readers will expect us to give account of the relationships because it is history that is being told. These stories must be told about future events and remembered by generations to come. These stories are apparatuses of Americo-Liberian history and what development were provided. What about those of us who were born tribal and act like it? Are there not stories about us to be told?

In their schemes, the Americo-Liberians would fabricate lies against African-Liberians who attempt to remind them about the dissatisfaction of the Natives and often put them in prisons. They would do everything to make such a person insignificant in the eyes of the Liberian public. This strategy reminds most Liberians about the proverb that says," Empty drum makes the loud noise." The fact of the matter is, when one has nothing valuable to contribute to a discussion, the only way out to rain insults on their opponents. Similarly, the Americo-Liberian leaders at the time could go to the extent of raining insults and referring to their opponents as being involved in tribalism, and sometimes they attempted to murder them.

A classic example of these behaviors were exemplified during a campaign for the presidency between President William Vacanarat Shadrach Tubman, an Americo-Liberian and Didhwo Tweh, a native Liberian. Tubman threatened to imprison him should he not behave in a civilized manner. Tweh's only crime was the challenge he pose to Mr. Tubman for the Liberian presidency.

Mutua (2006) confirmed that during Tubman's first term, Tweh supported him. Those who knew the both men considered them not only as friends but they were contributors to Tubman's famous Unification Policy. According to available literature, when Tubman was first elected, he was supported by Tweh and other indigenous people who felt that the Tubman Administration could bring about the needed changes that they long awaited. They believed that Tubman could bring the changes because of the positive relationship that Tubman had with the indigenous population. For example, in Maryland County, Tubman was considered a friend to the poor. He was known by some people as "Poor man Lawyer" because he represented free of charge those who could not afford to pay a lawyer's fee. But when Tubman became president, little did the indigenous people know that all along Tubman had other motives that were not in their best interests.

In addition, due to the slow pace of reform and the methods by which the True Whig Party (TWP) was going about to fully include the indigenous people into the mainstream activities of the Government of Liberia brought about opposition to Tubman Administration. The group of indigenous people did so by forming a political party called the Reformation Party of which Didhwo Tweh was elected as its standard bearer.

During the 1951 Presidential Campaign, one political commentator wrote, "Didhwo Twe, a Kru was running against Tubman for the presidency, used an old distinction to rally his followers. President, William V. S. Tubman in his campaign speech during an election eve broadcast referred to Tweh as being not only a member of the aborigines but charged him of trying to destabilized the Government. Tubman indicted Tweh as being supercilious misconceived notion and against the Government.

On the other hand, Mr. Tweh and his dangling group of the Kru supporters complain that for hundred and forty (140) years of the independence of Liberia, no aborigine (indigenous Liberian) have had the honor of being President of our common Nation. They claimed that from Joseph Jenkins Roberts, Stephen Allen Benson, Daniel Bashiel Warner, Edward James Roye, James Skiving Smith, Anthony William Gardiner, Alfred Francis Russ, Hilary Richard Wright Johnson, Joseph James Cheeseman, William David Coleman, Garretson Wilmot Gibson, Arthur Barclay, Charles Dunbar Burgess King, Edwin Barclay down to William V. S. Tubman were all Americo-Liberians. The aborigine people of this country were all born, bred and reared in Liberia but none could become president of their own Country.

The Americo-Liberian leadership (Presidents) before the 1980 military coup were as follows:

1. Joseph Jenkins Roberts 1848-1856
   - Born in Virginia, USA
   - First President of Liberia
   - Was elected six times

2. Stephen Allen Benson 1856-1864
   - Born in Maryland, USA
   - Second President of Liberia
   - Was elected four times

3. Daniel Bashiel Warner 1864-1868
   - Born in Maryland, USA
   - Third President of Liberia
   - Was elected twice

4. James Spriggs Payne 1868-1870
   - Born in Virginia, USA
   - Fourth President of Liberia
   - Was elected twice (2nd term: 1876-1878)

5. Edward James Roye 1870-1871
    - Born in Ohio, USA
    - Fifth President of Liberia
    - Was elected once
    - First President who was deposed in a coup d'état
    - First President who was assassinated

6. James Skivring Smith. Completed Roye's term 1871-1872
    - Born in South Carolina, USA
    - 6th President of Liberia
    - Serve the shortest term in the history of Liberia (two months)

7. Joseph Jenkins Roberts 1872-1876
    - Born in Virginia, USA,
    - 7th President of Liberia

8. James Spriggs Payne1876-1878, Second term 1976-1978
    - Born in Virginia, USA
    - 2nd term 1976-1978
    - 8th President of Liberia

9. Anthony William Gardiner 1878-1883
    - Born in Virginia, USA
    - 9th President of Liberia
    - Was elected three times
    - First President who resigned

10. Alfred Francis Russell completed Gardiner's term 1883-1884
    - Born in Kentucky, USA
    - 10th President of Liberia

11. Hilary Richard Wright Johnson 1884-1892 (First born in Africa)
    - Born in Monrovia, Monserrado County Liberia.
    - 11th President of Liberia
    - Was elected four times

12. Joseph James Cheeseman 1892-1896
    - Born in Edina, Grand Bassa County, Liberia
    - 12th President of Liberia
    - Was elected three times
    - First President who died in office

13. William David Coleman (VP) completed Cheeseman's term 1896-1900
    - Born in Kentucky, USA
    - 13rd President of Liberia0
    - Was elected twice
    - Second President who resigned.

14. Garretson Wilmot Gibson completed Coleman's term 1900-1904
    - Born in Maryland, USA
    - 14th President of Liberia
    - Was elected once

15. Arthur Barclay 1904-1912
    - Born in Bridgetown, Barbados, West Indies
    - 15th President of Liberia
    - Was elected three times
    - First President who served a four-year term

16. Daniel Edward Howard 1912-1920
    - Born in Buchanan, Grand Bassa County, Liberia
    - 16th President of Liberia
    - Was elected twice

17. Charles Dunbar Burgess King 1920-1930
    - Born in Freetown, Sierra Leone migrated to Liberia with his Sierra Leonean parents
    - 17th President of Liberia
    - Was elected three times
    - Third President who resigned

18. <u>Edwin James Barclay</u> completed King's term 1930-1944
    - Born in Brewerville, Montserrado County, Liberia
    - 18th President of Liberia
    - Was elected twice
    - First President who served an eight-year term

19. <u>William Vacanarat Shadrach Tubman 1944-1971</u>
    - Born in Harper, Maryland County, Liberia
    - 19th President of Liberia
    - Was elected six successive times
    - Longest serving President in Liberian history
    - Second President who died in office

20. <u>William Richard Tolbert, Jr. 1971-1980</u>
    - Born in Bensonville, Montserrado County, Liberia
    - 20th President of Liberia
    - Was elected once
    - Second President who was deposed in a coup
    - Second President, who was assassinated.

21. <u>Samuel Kanyon Doe -1985-1990</u>
    - Born in Tuzon, grand Gedeh County, Liberia
    - The third President who was assassinated
    - First elected Indigenous President

22. <u>Ellen Johnson-Sirleaf 2006-2017</u>
    - Born in Monrovia, Monserrado County
    - First elected female president
    - Elected for the second time

    Intern Presidents of Liberia
    - <u>Samuel Kanyon Doe (April 1980-Dec 1985)</u>
    - Amos Sawyer (November 1990 – August 1993)
    - Bismarck Kuyon (August 1993 – November 1993)
    - Philip Banks (November 1993 – February 1994)
    - David Kpormakor (Feb. 1994 – September 1995)
    - Wilton Sankawulo (Sept. 1995 – September 1996)

- <u>Ruth Perry (September 1996 – August 1997)</u> First female Head of State
- <u>Charles Gyude Bryant</u> (Oct. 2003 - January 16, 2006

The indigenous people came up with the distinctions. They claimed to have nothing to do with "THE LOVE OF LIBERTY BROUGHT US HERE" which excluded the natives who were on the land before Americo-Liberians came. This kind of attitude exists today whenever the mistreatment of African-Liberians is being discussed in political cycles. For example, an individual is accused of practicing tribalism if the person supports the individual from his/her tribe that possesses the requisite qualifications and skills for a particular position. I don't see the reason why an indigenous person should be accused of engaging in tribalism when they support their indigenous citizen. In short, Americo-Liberian rule was characterized by brutality, corruption, exploitation, human rights abuses and mismanagement of public resources.

African-Liberian cultural and religious practices will have to be respected in the same way the cultural and religious practices of Americo-Liberians are respected. Moreover, Liberia will be doomed should there be any attempt to return to the Americo-Liberian Plantation hegemony, which will again subject the indigenous African to second class status.

CHAPTER FOUR

TREATMENTS MELTED ON THE INDIGENOUS-LIBERIANS BY LIBERIAN LEADERS

Suppression was a part of the history and political legacy of Liberia since the founding of the country and throughout Americo-Liberian rule from which Doe may have acquired his oppressive style of dictatorship. These historical events showed that the suppressions, executions of politicians, election irregularities, and control of opposition leaders through brutal force existed in Liberian politics long before President Doe and the 1980 military coup which executed thirteen prominent True Whig Party leaders.

4.1 Treatments melted the Country (Indigenous) people

The treatments of slaves in the United States was generally characterized by brutality, degradation, and inhumanity which were practiced by the Americo-Liberian leaders, Whippings, executions, and rapes were commonplace. Similarly, the indigenous Liberians were punished by whipping, shackling, hanging, beating, and imprisonment. For example, the Lawyers Committee for Human Rights Reports (1986) indicated that in Liberia, the "years of settlers' rule were characterized by severe exploitation of the indigenous inhabitants" (p. 12). During President Edward J. Barclay's administration in 1938, seven famous Gbandi tribal chiefs including Gbandi Chief, Mbabulu Vonjoe) were rounded up and ordered them buried alive in a mass grave for refusing to take orders and directives from an Americo-Liberian Government. The report indicated that instead of allowing the chiefs the opportunity to defend themselves in a trial, they were put in a mass grave in order to set an example for the rest of the tribal people that they should not disobey the Americo-Liberians.

Punishment was most often meted on African opposition politicians in response to political challenges and disobedience or even perceived infractions, or simply to re-assert the dominance of the Americo-Liberian Leadership over the African; like the white slave masters did to Black slave women. For example, indigenous men were deployed in the army—formerly the Liberian Frontier Force—to forcibly collect taxes from their African brothers for a government in which they were not represented or allowed to participate.

In like manner, Richardson (1959) pointed out that another example was in the hinterland; the indigenous people were forcibly recruited to perform government public works to build and maintain public roads as well as to work on the plantations of some Americo-Liberians without pay. These treatment were another form of slavery practiced by descendants of former American slaves.

In the case of the American Slavery, all the slave "Master" wanted was to get off quick, so all he had to do is open his pants, have the woman bend over or lean against a tree or fence, and he do it. A "Quickie" was done ANYWHERE at ANYTIME! Any place the master wanted it, it could even happen out in public but it surely would not happen in a nice, comfortable bed in the master's house.

4.2 Liberia: Africa's First Republic

Archeologically, Liberia occupies a unique place in the political history of Africa for three important reasons among others:

(a) First, Liberia is the oldest republic in the continent, dating back to 1847.
(b) Until 1984, Liberia boasted of being the oldest de facto one political party system that worked in Africa, as the then ruling True Whig Party (TWP) had been in power continuously since 1877 to 1980.

(c) Liberia was the only country in Africa that did not experience a European style of colonization unlike its neighbors of Guinea, Ivory Coast, and Sierra Leone.

The American and European politicians felt that the "freed men of color" as they were called, had become a serious social and economic burden on the white dominated society of Europe and the United States. In Liberia, the Americo-Liberian held unto political power, which sored the seed of conflict in Liberia.

4.3 Characteristics of Governance and Life in Liberia

The methods of governance in Liberia has been one of the obstacles in to sustainable development. As stated in other sections of this book, the Americo-Liberian rules were characterized by brutality, corruption, exploitation, human rights abuses, and mismanagement of public resources. The year 1964 was the first time in the history of Liberia that the hinterland people -the indigenous- were represented in the National Legislature of Liberia.

This was another form of slavery practiced by descendants of former American slaves all of which contributed to the underdevelopment of the Country.

Further, the establishment of Liberia and the leadership that followed thereafter became one of the prime causes of the Liberia's underdevelopment. In facts, the 1847 Constitution excluded the Native African and Liberian women from participation in the Government. The Natives and women were not allowed to vote or be voted for in any elected position. Although, agriculture was the major occupation of the majority of Liberians but most farmers engaged in subsistence farming of upland rice, cassava, yam, peanuts, sugarcane, and assorted vegetables. The principal commercial activity has been cash tree crops — rubber, cocoa, coffee, and palm products. The mining of iron ore has been the country's dominant mining industry. Beyond these activities, employment by the government was the major source of paid employment. Therefore, economic deprivation or depriving the non-Americo-Liberian majority of the right to employment with the government further became factors to discontents and led to underdevelopment of the Nation.

The alteration of African boundaries by European colonial countries in creating states in sub-Saharan Africa has negatively affected the stability of these countries. In a similar way, the establishment of Liberia divided the African tribes among two or more neighboring countries. For example, there are Kissi, Lorma, Mandingo, and Kpelle living in Liberia, Guinea, and Sierra Leone. The Gio were divided between Guinea and Liberia, while the Kissi and Mende tribes were distributed between Liberia and Sierra Leone. The Mano, Kru, and Krahn were allocated between the Ivory Coast and Liberia. The lack of consideration for cultural, linguistic, social, and economic differences and values of the Africans before integrating them into a nation-state created ethnic conflicts in the regions. These integrations resulted in mistrust, which, has been one of the instigating factors in the lack of development, especially in the case of Liberia, where the Americo-Liberians held cultural, social, and political dominance for 133 years.

The Liberian government recognized sixteen (16) ethnic groups of indigenous Africans in addition to the descendants of free blacks from the Western hemisphere.

These ethnic groups were the Bassa, Belle, Dey, Gbandi, Gio, Gola, Grebo, Kissi, Kpelle, Krahn, Kru, Lorma, Mano, Mende, Sarpo and Vai. They spoke different languages and comprised 95% of the population, yet the Americo-Liberians, the 5% of the population who could not speak any of the African languages, imposed English as the official language for governmental business, formal education, and the mass media. The traditional education and cultural format of the natives was not only unacceptable but was condemned by the Settlers and referred to them as devils. I have understood from these and other experiences that when the majority of the citizens are imposed upon, they will usually revolt against their oppressors, which becomes a prime factor for further conflict. In the case of Liberia, the ethnic groups or indigenous Africans opposed the Americo-Liberians' domination.

As Sawyer (1992) stressed, the African majority in Liberia came to perceive the Americo-Liberians to be no better than the European colonizers. Many indigenous Liberian felt that if the Europeans must give up control in Africa, Liberia's own oppressors — the settlers – must do likewise. This notion, was the beginning of internal ethnic conflict in Liberia. For example, as Sawyer (1992) indicated, the Dey and Gola war of 1822, the Vai uprising of 1850, the Grebo war of 1856, the Kru irredentism of 1930, and the Rice Demonstration of 1979, among others were all intended to put an end to Americo-Liberian domination.

4.4 Impacts of Elections on the Underdevelopment Liberia

Historical events showed that Liberian elections have been marked by frauds and corruptions from the time of the first Americo-Liberian rule to the present Ellen Johnson-Sirleaf administration in Liberia. These fraudulent practices have been one of the major causes of lack of both physical and human development.

Marinelli (1964) cited as an example the 1926 presidential election, during which time Pres. Charles C. D. King was opposed by Thomas J. Faulkner, a fearless politician and a friend to the natives. In Grand Bassa County at the time, there were 3,000 legal voters (the women and the indigenous population were not allowed to vote), yet 32,000 people registered to vote and 72,000 people voted. The results of the 1926 election credited Faulkner's People's Party with 8,500 votes and 63,500 for King's True Whig Party.

As Marinelli (1964) pointed out, when the issue was contested in court, the judge appointed by the True Whig Party denied the protest; nevertheless, the case was sent on appeal to the Supreme Court where it created embarrassment for the judiciary. They fined the lower court judge $150 and the election sheriff $50. The legislature was compelled by international pressure to recount the ballots, but before the recount began, they discovered stacks of unfolded ballots and several burned ballot boxes. President King was declared the winner and succeeded himself.

Another historical example is that when Pres. Edward J. Roye's term of office was to end January 1, 1872, according to Nelson (1984), he issued a proclamation extending the tenure of his presidency for another two years without an election. His authority was challenged, but his followers promised to stand by him in his constitutional act to change the term of the presidency from two years to four years.

Liebenow (1969) cited as an example the 1943 presidential during which election, Tubman, a Supreme Court justice was selected by his friend, Edward J. Barclay, to succeed him; a practice known in Liberian politics as the "spoils system." Tubman was opposed by an experienced Democratic Party leader, James F. Cooper, a former secretary of the interior, but the TWP refused to allow Cooper's observers at the voting booths. After the election returns were counted, Liebenow (1969) claimed, a small village of about twenty-four huts in Marshall Territory with a population of less than 1,000 people, including men, women, children, and their domesticated animals, was credited with 5,100 votes for Tubman's TWP and 7 votes in favor of Cooper.

Tubman was declared the winner without a chance for redress, confrontation, or confirmation. These events in Liberian political history are confirmations in explaining how the methods of governance and political repression were imbedded in the minds of the Liberian people and even how young politicians now believed that dishonesty was a better path to political success in Liberia. In subsequent elections of President Tubman, one individual could vote as many times as the person is able to stand in line and vote. There were no true oppositions to contest the results of elections.

President Doe's administration should also be blamed for Liberia's underdevelopment because of his rigging of the 1985 presidential and general elections. His lack of tolerance for opposition leaders, and his oppression, among other reasons all causes for the underdevelopment and the level of poverty. Given that Doe stole the 1985 election as claimed, history tells us that there has never been any fair election in Liberia, in a democratic manner, fair and transparent at least based on the constitution of the country, from Joseph Jenkins Roberts, the first president of the Americo-Liberian hegemony, to William Richard Tolbert, the last. In addition, several indigenous people learned from the tricks of the Americo-Liberians that the best path to success in Liberian politics was through fraudulent tactics and dishonest strokes which do not promote development.

Recent examples of election fraud in Liberia were the general elections that were held in the country on October 15, 1985, and the one held in October 2011 election. The 1985 election was the first elections since the April 12, 1980, coup that brought the People's Redemption Council (PRC) into power. The hopes for the elections were high on all sides. Official announcements indicated that the National Democratic Party won the presidential election with 50.93 percent of the vote. This numbers were just enough to avoid a runoff election. The major opposition candidate or the standard bearer of Liberia Action Party who was allocated 26.45 percent and Liberia Unification Party and Unity Party were both apportioned eleven point 11.55 percent and 11.07 percent, respectively. President Doe's party won large majorities in both houses of the lawmaking body. The Liberian

Action Party won few senatorial seats, but the party leaders advised their partisans not to take their position in the National Legislature, including Ellen Johnson-Sirleaf.

The polls were tarnished by accusations of widespread fraud and rigging of the election. There may have been some credibility to these assertions which stained both parties of the two Does (Samuel K. Doe and Jackson F. Doe—they were not related) who participated in the election. Many independent observers believed that Jackson Doe, who officially finished second, was the actual winner of the election. It was later discovered that Samuel Doe had the ballots re-marked in a secret location between Kakata and the Bong Mines Company by his party chairman's handpicked staff. The votes for opposition candidates were removed and replaced by their own marked ballots in favor of Pres. Samuel K. Doe's National Democratic Party of Liberia.

There were also credible information that Liberia Action Party had planted pool workers and paid them money to stuff extra ballots in favor of their party, particularly in the Monrovia and Firestone concession areas. These contentions were supported by video recordings that were displaced by the then chairman of the National Election Commission. In any case, the ballots were later brought in Monrovia to be publicly counted in the presence of the press and cameras. When the government was installed, the country saw increased tribal tensions, which ultimately led to the start of the national civil conflict in 1989 and Doe's overthrow and subsequent killing in 1990 instead of focusing on the development of the Country.

The election of the first female President of Liberia was not without fraud. The election also brought lingering bitterness with her opponents, led by Winston Tubman of the Congress for Democratic Change. The challenger who withdrew from the runoff in November claiming fraud in the first round the month before. Political analyst believed that the President and supporters with the assistance of the National Election Commission developed several strategies to ridge the election.

Some believed that extra ballots were printed and given to strong supporters who cashed ballots in-favor of the President Johnson-Sirleaf's Unity Party. They claimed that President extended the period of voters registration for extra weeks, contrary to the election guidelines in order to allow them time to register extra voter registrations. These extra voter registration cords were given to strong partisans of the Unity Party to put in votes for their party. For example, in Kolahun District, Kolba City, Electrical District number three, a member of Unity Party was found with more than two hundred (200) voter registration cards in his pockets. The issue was reported to the Election Magistrate among other complains who had engineered the strategies but there was no redress. They claimed that another version was that special arrangements were made with the ballot printers who use special inks on the ballots that would get dry within one to two hours after voting. These ballots were distributed only in strong holds areas of the opponents thereby increasing in huge number of invalid votes. Meanwhile, international observers were quick to praise the election as being free and fair in order to maintain the fragile peace. The runoff election was tarnished by an opposition boycott and street clashes between protesters and the police. The turnout in the runoff dropped by half. Whatever took place, the truth is to be established.

The two days before the vote, Winston Tubman's supporters clashed with the police, who responded with tear gas and gunfire. At least one person died and several others were injured. The cleavages that led to decades of civil war still run deep in the Country. During a speech in the United States, President Sirleaf freely and openly admitted that there were frauds in the election. She cited as an example that her Market Women Association Members took voting card of their children to stop them from voting for her opponents.

Mr. Winston Tubman and other leaders of his party, the Congress for Democratic Change decided to boycott President Johnson-Sirleaf's inauguration. They vowed to neither recognize nor cooperate with the new administration but ultimately Tubman announced the day before inauguration that they would attend. Despite the violence and boycott, President Johnson Sirleaf's election showed that she is the only female elected President of Liberia for an independent Country founded by freed American slaves since 1847.

The Liberian situation has produced a delinquent subculture oriented toward confessions. The disregard for the integration of the indigenous population into the political life of the country and an emphasis on the role of power and coercion by the ruling class has left many Liberians confused without special divinities. Children of the indigenous Liberian were sent to live with Americo-Liberians as wards- who took the last names of their masters.

4.5 How Superiority and Suppression Caused of Underdevelopment?

There are many factors that contributed and caused the underdevelopment of the Liberia but before we can discuss the factors that have relative levels of influence on Liberia's own experiences and the causes of underdevelopment or backwardness of the country in terms of human, educational, health and physical development such as roads, buildings, and resource, we must first briefly examine Liberia's unique history.

Based on the system of racial segregation in the United States of America, the Americo-Liberians recreated a cultural and social caste system with themselves at the top and indigenous Liberians at the bottom. They did not believe in a form of equality with the natives. The natives all had the potential to become "civilized" only through conversion to Christianity and western education.

Liberia gained its independence in 1847, making it the first and oldest independent African republic. The nation's founding fathers and first set of leaders unfortunately failed to set a clear vision of inclusive political, social and economic governance of the new nation-the Liberian State, leading to a path of social, political and economic segregation and discrimination, where the indigenous population were marginalized for more almost a century.

As world history has told us repeatedly – especially most recently in the Middle East – marginalized societies tend to fight back against the system suppressing them. At the same time, the elite or privileged class will do all they can to maintain the status quo because of the enormous benefits they and their families and cronies enjoy. The Liberian situation accordingly, is no exception. As more and more indigenous Liberians and their sympathizers gained formal education and enlightenments, after many years following independence, the indigenous people revolted against the elite, leading to the 1979 Rice Riot, the 1980 Military Coup d' tat and the 1989 civil war, which lasted for more than 14 years, claiming thousands of lives and displacing others both internally and externally in the process.

As indicated elsewhere, from time of independence in 1847 to April 12, 1980 the presidents were all Americo-Liberians and none was an indigenous Liberian. Further, eleven (11) of the nineteenth presidents were actually born in the United States of America. They viewed themselves first as Americans before Liberian citizens because in the American Constitution, it is stated that any one born in America is a citizen of the United States of America. Accordingly, they paid little or no attention to sustainable development of Liberia and the sensibilities of the indigenous Liberians with regard to their customs, laws, and religious beliefs. In addition, before 1946, Liberia had two separate laws: one for the indigenous Liberians and the other set governed Americo-Liberians who occupied the coastal area of the country.

The aborigines of this country were always here and did not come from any other country yet they could not become presidents of their own land. The Americo-Liberians perpetuated themselves in political, social and economic powers. For example, Liberia's 18th President William V.S. Tubman, lasted in power for 27 years (1944-1971), He was only removed from office by death.

President, William V. S. Tubman
He served the longest terms (1944-1971)
He was called Father of modern Liberia

During the 1960s and the first half of the 1970s, the iron ore sector attracted substantial foreign investors and by 1975, Liberia had become the world's fifth largest exporter of iron ore. Moreover, from 1946 to 1972, the Tubman Administration also attracted huge amount of foreign investments yet Liberia did not have any sustainable development. This immense economic growth, which was rivaled only by Japan at the time, was considered by many people as a miracle. There was no execuse for the lack of development during this period. This was a missed opportunities: just as Clower et. al. (1966) recognized, there were growth without development, particularly during the Tubman's administration. Unfortunately, this remarkable and miraculous economic growth that took place in Liberia was not translated into economic, social or physical development. They further became prime factor for future political and social instability and the subsequently led to more than 14-year civil conflict from 1989 to 2003 which hindered development in Liberia.

The book discovered that President, William Richard Tolbert, the country's nineteenth presidents (from 1947 to April 12, 1980), was assassinated through a military coup was also very corrupt, greedy, and oppressive.

The TWP under Tolbert's liberal concept was unable to respond fully to the political yearning of the educated and dedicated indigenous Liberians who were proud enough not to sell their "birthrights" to Americo-Liberian political hegemony. Among the indigenous Liberian people, there are considerable concerns as to whether the supports they received from the Tolbert government could be attributed to his multiple roles as President of Liberia, President of the World Baptist Convention, Chairman of the Organization of African Unity (OAU), Baptist Pastor and Grand Master of the Masonic Craft of Liberia.

Another related but more recent event took place when then vice president, William Richard Tolbert put in place a special exploitative arrangement with the former Gbandi Paramount Chief, the late Mbomoo-Yallah, who Milligan (1989) referred to as the owner of "human medicine," to provide free laborers on his estate. These arrangements were passed on to Chief Yallah's successor, Thomas Kollie, after Yallah's death in 1957.

Accordingly, a truck was usually sent for able men in Kolahun City, Lofa County and each of the ten clans at the time could select these men from their villages to be shipped to the vice president's farm to perform free labor. The town's people were required to provide food (rice and palm oil) for the men to eat during their three-month stay on the vice president's plantation. At the end of the three-month period, they were not allowed to return home in the same truck that went for their replacements. Therefore, the trucks usually went empty to bring replacement workers. Hence, these men had to earn money by working either on Tolbert's farm for less pay or at the American Firestone rubber plantation in order to go back to their homes.

Tessler (2009) admitted that President Tolbert, like President Taylor did not hesitate to spend money freely from the government treasury on projects that were in his personal interest, such as paving the road to his family home in Bentol. Tolbert also changed the name of the city from Bensonville to Bentol in order to add the first three letters of his family. He also declared his birthday a national holiday in Liberia and called it "Rally time" day.

In Lofa County, particularly the Gbande Tribes, when the leaders or Government officers visit their areas, they expected not only to provide them with food and accommodations, but to gown them with country clothes. During the latter part of President Tubman's administration, Vice President Tolbert opened rice and clothing stores in each of the four new Counties at the time of Lofa, Bong, Nimba and Grand Gedeh Counties. It became mandatory for such gift and rice to be purchased only from the Vice President's Store, as they were called. A chief buying rice or clothes from any other store was required to pay the Vice President's store twice the value of the commodities that was not purchased form his store. These behaviors and actions represented personal greed for political and economic power.

The political situation in modern Liberia was a serious risk even during the regime of Pres. William V. S. Tubman, particularly in the 1950s. For example, Williams (2002) stated that an indigenous journalist, Tuan Wreh, was imprisoned during the presidential campaign between his independent party and Tubman's party the True Whig Party (TWP)—for writing an article explaining why citizens should vote for his independent party and not for Tubman. This article led to Tuan Wreh's arrest on accusations of libel and defamation of character, for which he was jailed for five months, though he was never been taken to court or formally charged. Before the five months ended, he was summoned by the national legislature, only to be told by the speaker of the House of Representatives, "Go in peace and sin no more."

Similarly, according to Williams (2002), another citizen, Rufus Darpoh, was wrongly accused by President, Doe's administration and sent to Belle Yalla's notorious prison for six months. Like Tuan Wreh, Darpoh was advised by the Executive Mansion after three months in jail that God had given him long life but he had been careless with it, and he was set free.

Lawyers Committee on Human Rights Report (1986) indicated that the struggle between the Americo-Liberians and the African majority came to its logical conclusion in the bloody assassination of President William

Richard Tolbert on April 12, 1980 by M/Sgt. Samuel K. Doe and sixteen noncommissioned army officers. The ringleaders of the coup were all young indigenous African soldiers, lacking experiences beyond their basic military service. Doe and his followers were from six of the sixteen tribes who took arms in a dramatic military coup that toppled the Americo-Liberian regime. One of the intentions of the military coup was to put an end to what they called rampant corruption, misuse of public funds, and stop suppression of the Africans whom the Americo-Liberians met on the land.

4.6 How the Military Coup and Civil Wars Hindered Development in Liberia

Deng (1996) described, the acts of the revolutions that brought independence to most of Africa in the 1960s, also caused acts of ethnic violence in Liberia beyond comparison. The Lawyers Committee on Human Rights Report (1986) indicated that the struggle between the Americo-Liberians and the African majority came to its logical conclusion in the bloody assassination of President William Richard Tolbert by Master Sergeant Samuel K. Doe and 16 non commissioned army officers. The ringleaders of the coup were all young indigenous African soldiers, lacking experiences beyond their basic military service. Doe and his followers were from six (6) of the sixteen (16) tribes who took arms in a dramatic military coup that toppled the Americo-Liberian regime.

Master Sergeant, CIC and President, Samuel K. Doe
He executed 13 members of the Former TWP Government

On April 22, 1980, ten days after the coup, twenty-eight-year-old M/Sgt. Samuel K. Doe, acting as chairman of the People's Redemption Council (PRC) and head of state and government, ordered the execution of thirteen of the most prominent members of the former regime who were all Americo-Liberians. The order was carried out by a firing squad before television cameras, despite several appeals for clemency from the Organization of African Unity (OAU), the Economic Community of West African States (ECOWAS), and the United States government.

The supporters of the PRC claimed that the executions were not only necessary to put an end to the new forms of slavery established by descendants of former slaves but were also called for as the people who were executed had both financial resources and international contacts which could be used to hire mercenaries to fight them. CIC Doe and his followers felt that the former government officers could use their ill-gotten wealth and international connections to remove the military government from powers.

Doe's government promised to liberate the indigenous population from oppression by the Americo-Liberians, to stamp out corruption, and to put an end to the economic and political domination by the elite settlers. The PRC also promised to establish a more equitable distribution of the nation's wealth among all Liberians.

On the contrary, once the coup was successful in toppling the regime of the Americo-Liberians, the victors, the PRC found themselves repeating the same vicious cycle of repression and oppression that the Americo-Liberians had done. The PRC's oppressive actions and failed promises to heal the wounds inflicted on the ethnic groups by Americo-Liberian regimes became yet another factor contributing to the Underdevelopment and poverty in the Country. The PRC members illogically promoted themselves in the Liberian army.

The inhumane acts of the PRC was one of the reasons Doe's government experienced attempted coups—more than any other regime in the history of Liberia. Many military personnel, especially those from other ethnic groups, believed that if a master sergeant from a small, marginalized ethnic group such as the Krahns could lead a successful coup and rule the nation, so they too might do the same.

As time passed, President Doe's government responded to coup attempts with extreme brutality and summary executions. Most of the other ringleaders of the original 1980 coup were later killed for attempted coups against their own government, including Doe's two vice presidents, Thomas Weh Syen and J. Nicholas Poodier, and the commanding general of the Armed Forces of Liberia, Thomas G. Quiwonkpa. These events were overall causes of underdevelopment of Liberia.

The Liberian Civil War began on December 24, 1989, when a small band of rebels led by President Doe's former procurement chief, Charles Taylor, invaded Liberia from Côte d'Ivoire. Taylor and his National Patriotic Front rebels rapidly gained the support of Liberians and some people in the international communities because of the repressive nature of Pres. Samuel Doe and his government. Barely six months after the rebels first attacked, they reached the outskirts of Monrovia.

The first and second Liberian civil wars were Africa's bloodiest and destructive wars, which claimed the lives of more than two hundred thousand Liberians and displaced a million others into refugee camps. All these people could have contributed to the development of the Country. In addition, the Economic Community of West African States (ECOWAS) intervened and spent millions of dollars to maintain the soldiers which amount could have used for development of African first republic

Prince Johnson who had been a member of Taylor's National Patriotic Front of Liberia (NPFL) but broke away because of policy differences, formed the Independent National Patriotic Front of Liberia (INPFL). Johnson's forces captured and killed President Doe on September 9, 1990.

Initially, it was widely believed among the Americo-Liberian sector in Liberia that President Reagan and Vice President Bush's administration had created President Doe and later made him appear as an invincible dictator to the Liberian people. This propaganda, according to them, was effected through the intelligence network of the United States CIA and was supported by the preponderance of foreign aid provided to the Doe regime from 1980–1990. They maintained that these foreign aids were more than all the aid provided to Tubman and Tolbert combined. On the other hand, the United States, turned its back on the President Doe's government during the civil war. The 14 years of senseless civil war was a major hindrance to development in Liberia and its neighbors.

Darkortey (2007) indicated that bad policies, lack of policies and policies inconsistencies are undermining development in Liberia. He claimed that ill policies are continuously reducing the life expectancy of Liberians as a result of poverty, disease, and the hard laborious jobs they secure with companies like Firestone and, perhaps, Mittal Steel to come.

Let us face it, a 30 years old uneducated Flomo who resides in a village of Bong County is less healthy than a 30 years old educated Nimely who resides in Monrovia, while a 30 years old educated American is much more healthier and stands to live longer than members of his age grouping found in Liberia. The lower life expectancy of the country is an example of these continuous ill policies that are killing Liberians before they can grow.

Darkortey (2007) believed that another evidence of these wrong policies is that after more than 200 years of existence, Liberia still chronically lacks infrastructure development, thus coercing her citizens to live dismally, lacks functioning road networks which facilitate the movements of people and goods and services. Consequently, he claimed that the economy is weak because there are no markets for some goods and services since the infrastructure that brings buyers and sellers together are lacking. Darkortey (2007) maintained that the prime examples of bad policies, lack of policies, and policies inconsistencies are Liberia's failures to build and maintain road network or even just to fill the highways with dirty that is washed away during the rainy season. The country completely lacks policies to build, connect, and maintain its road infrastructure as can be seen by the lack of such infrastructure.

4.7 Collection of Tax From the indigenous People

The **hut tax** was a type of taxation introduced by European colonialists in Africa and as payment of taxes per hut or household basis. It was originally payable in money, labor, grain or stock and benefited only the colonial authorities. In Liberia, the Americo-Liberians instructed members of the Arm Forces (Liberian Frontier Forces) to forcibly collected taxes from their indigenous brothers for a government that they were not allowed to be a part. The soldiers placed men who did not have the money to pay in the sun light and forced to watch the sun until the money is paid by their families. Others whose families could not raise money were either beaten, their head put in hot waters or placed in the sun for several days.

The issue of reintroduction was discussed by the Liberian Government, it was proposed that hut tax must not be reintroduced because of the injustices and cruelty that was associated with its collection, partially forming a pretext to violence in this country. Dr. Togba Nah Tipoteh, chairman of the Steering Committee of Vision 2030, warned that re-introduction of the 'hut tax' in Liberia, abolished since 1980, would "exacerbate poverty and instigate violence" in the country. *Boima J. V. Boima* also indicated that households which had survived the brutality of the Americo-Liberian rule in the process of hut tax collection, stored their wealth in cattle- ranching or sent member of their families to work on Americo-Liberian plantations or in Firestone in order to raise cash with which to pay the hut tax.

Another situation that was eradicated by the Americo-Liberian rule was the "pawn system." This was the practice of chiefs of certain tribes to send children of their tribe to coastal Americo-Liberian tribes for work for payment to the chief. By stopping this practice, the interior tribes said they could not generate money for the hut tax. Further, the carriers, formally pawns, refused to work for the one shilling per day wage. These practices were later modified to domestic servants. This became a practice in which an indigenous child would live with an Americo-Liberian family, serve as domestic servant- or house boy or girl as the case may be without pay in change for feeding the child. Some of these Americo-Liberian families could allow the child to take their last names, get education at a minimum level. The children of the indigenous Liberians were not allowed to attend the same schools as the children of the Americo-Liberians.

In addition, Americo-Liberian economy depended upon Indigenous Africans' labor to build new roads or maintain existing ones as well as construct government houses in rural Liberia. Many of the public high ways in the interior part of Liberia were constructed by the indigenous labor using holes and diggers, without compensation or pay. Male adult were recruited and forced to work on the public road and public buildings without compensation. In many of the instances, these men take with them food from their towns and villages to eat while constructing the public highways. in the political headquarters. A man who refused to work were either whipped, or imprisoned for a period of three month.

4.8 Travels of Americo-Liberian in the Hinterland

It was the policy of the Americo-Liberian administration that whenever government official travelled, he or she was taken on the head of indigenous Liberians in hummocks from one town/village to another. The personal properties of their bodyguard (soldier) were also transported from villagers. The men from one village were required to take their bags from their town or village to the next town. In addition, each soldier in the

Americo-Liberian Government was entitled to a rooster, fifteen cups of rice and a quart of palm oil whether or not they sleep in a town or village. Many of these soldiers were indigenous Liberians who were instructed to patrol from one village to another, either to collect hut tax or to bring about awareness that the payment of hut taxes were expected. Usually, the soldiers were encouraged to take these trips because of the food and other commodities they obtained during these official trips. These practices continued until President Tolbert administration abolished it.

4.9 The Term of Office for Presidents in Liberia

In 1847 the President's term of office was two years. During the Administration of President Arthur Barclay the term of office was changed to four years, in 1907. His cousin President Edwin Barclay changed it to eight years, in 1936. It was restored to four years in 1950 under President Tubman - was elected a record number of consecutive six times. During the Tolbert Administration, in 1976, it was again changed to eight years. Under 1986 Constitution of Liberia, the term of office was change to six years to succeed once. At present the presidential term of office still remains six years whereas the president can only succeed once.

The longest serving president in Liberian history was William V. S. Tubman, serving from 1944 until his death in 1971. The shortest term was held by James Skivring Smith, who was in office for (interim president) for two months. However, the political process from Liberia's founding in 1847, despite widespread corruption and oppressions, was stable until the end of the First Republic in 1980.

CHAPTER FIVE

RECOMMENDATIONS

The author of this book has addressed a wide range of rationales for the underdevelopment of Liberia such as stratifications between Liberian ethnic groups- Americo-Liberians and Indigenous Liberians, the formation of the country and the disparities in the political, social, and economic opportunities. The level of corruptions, mismanagement of the public resources, type of policies formulated by the leaders, and many other reasons for the underdevelopment of Liberia. According to World report (2015) the United States has the largest economy in the World. In 2012 the US economy was 18.87 percent of the World Total or $15.684 trillion and China was $12.405 trillion. Liberia had 162rd highest place in the World economy, about $318 million.

There is a great need for resources necessary for building a sustainable and sound development either by governments, international institutions and individuals as well as fostering a stable relationship to the rest of the Third World. Further, there are several lessons to be learned from the aggressions of a few powerful Liberians who have failed to develop the country but instead destroyed the country and denied the majority of the population. It is imperative that the Liberian people, the Liberian government, and the international community address issues that existed in Liberia such as bad policies, and segregations between the two group of citizens, event prior to the 1980 Military Coup and the National Civil Conflicts, especially the prime reasons or factors that led to the lack of development and the magnitude of poverty.

The country must support a vigorous effort in order to have post-conflict reconstruction, reestablish the political and social system in Liberia, and prevent a reoccurrence of these slave mentality. The Liberians must also address and discuss with each other post-conflict issues to ensure that the New Liberia will be based on sound principles and policies for restructuring the Liberian political, social and economic system. This concept of the New Liberia must entail a general participation in the political, economic, social, and technological systems of the country in tandem with the decentralization and democratization of the Liberian society. This means that in the New Liberia, the politicians, leaders, and decision makers must break away from the old habits of corruptions, mismanagement of public resources, inequalities in educational and medical opportunities and the practices of preferential treatment in allocating government opportunities. They must do away with the political and social alienation of one group of the society.

As discussed in Moniba's (1992) book: Liberian Politics Today, poverty and illiteracy were the underlining causes of the underdevelopment of Liberia. There should be new educational policies that will develop the human resources in the New Liberia. This policy must strive to provide equal educational opportunities, minimized or if possible eliminate illiteracy, and create an educated Liberian public. This concept should be embraced as a part of the post-war reconstruction programs which President Ellen Johnson-Sirleaf Government failed to carry through.

The image a government projects to the international communities determines its relationships to the rest of the World community and how it interacts with other governments. Therefore, the Liberian Government should improve its image through Liberia's foreign policies and its relationships with other nations. The prospects of developed Liberia greatly depend on the country's leadership and ability of the Liberian leaders to mobilize and coordinate international assistance in every form, especially from the United States because of the longstanding mutual relations between the two countries.

Since the civil conflict ended, Liberian expatriates have refrained from returning to their homeland because of the security situation. The New Liberia requires the establishment of modem security institutions with the improvement in the fundamental respect for human rights, especially a nation-building process that will lead to genuine peace, democracy and sustainable development as well as put an end to irresponsible actions by political power seekers.

The Liberian discriminatory rule has created many problems, raised several questions, and posed stiff challenges to the development of the Country. As Olsen (1996) noted, Liberia is so rich in natural beauty and resources that many scholars and academicians cannot help but wonder why such a nation is not developed instead its own citizens are bent on self-destruction. Further, the severity of the behavior of past political leaders makes one wonder what can be done so the Liberians people will cohabitate as equal in their destroyed homes. Still another important question is whether Liberians will ever live together as equal citizens and develop their common country. Despite the many traumas experienced by Liberians, (the rice riots, military coup and the two civil wars) there are reasons for hope that development, peace and stability will once more prevail in Liberia.

One of the realities that symbolizes the lack of development is that the country is losing the people with the talents and professionalism, who are capable of rebuilding the civil society. Many of the educated, trained and professional Liberians as well as experienced citizens are either dying in foreign lands or have established themselves without hopes or plans of returning to their country. The Liberian's hopes for peace and stability lies with the persevering, patriotic, adaptable, and determined citizens. One simple question that has never been fully answered is why were Americo-Liberian segregating and excluding their own brothers and sisters from the political and social activities of their Country?

In conclusion, one of the solutions to Liberia's problem lies in our ability to learn from our past experiences, learn to live together as coequals, have faith in our abilities and commitment to develop our country as well as the courage to create a new society with flourishing opportunities that will make Liberia less dependent on foreigners. The country needs a policy of inclusion and equal opportunity for all its citizens.

BIBLIOGRAPHY

Adams, G.S. (2000). *A Case Study: The Effect of Exposure to Multiple Intelligences Theory on High School Students*. Unpublished Doctoral Dissertation, Walden University)

Agbese, P. O (1996). *Ethnicity, Conflicts and Hometown Associations: An Analysis of the Experience of the Sigila Development Association*, Ikeja, Nigeria: Sahel

Aning, E.K. (1997). *The International Dimensions of Internal Conflict: The Case of Liberia and West Africa*. Copenhagen, Germany: Centre for Development Research.

Berman, B.J. (1995). *I, Patronage and African States: The Politics of Uncivil Nationalism in African Affairs*. Thousand Oaks, California: Sage Publications.

Bolton, B. (1995). *Just Keep on Walking: An African Odyssey*. Baton Rouge, Louisiana: Louisiana State University Press.

Casey, M.A. (2000). *Focus Groups: A Practical Guide for Applied Research*. (3rd edition), Thousand Oaks, California: Sage Publications.

Chieh, D.D. (2011). *Needles, Bullets and Knives: The Assassinations of Three Liberian Presidents- Memoirs of a Public Servant)*. Raleigh, North Carolina: Lulu Press, Inc.

Chayes, A. and Chayes, A.H. (1996). *Preventing Conflict in the Developing World: Mobilizing International and Regional Organizations.* Washington, DC: Brookings Institution.

Conteh-Morgan and Magyar (1998). *Peacekeeping in Africa: ECOMOG in Liberia.* New York, New York: St. Martin's.

Darkartey, R. (2007). Political Commentary and Reflection on Liberia. Cleveland, Ohio: Forest City Enterprises.

Dawson, J. (1999). How to Manage Conflict, Anger, and Emotions: Control, Confidence and Compassions even in the Most Highly Changed Situation. *International Journal of Social Science,* 9(2), 2-26.

Deng, F. M. (1996). Ethnicity: An African Predicament. *Social Science Review.* 9(3) 46-66.

Economic Community of West African States—ECOWAS –(1991). *The Liberian Conflict and its Impacts on the West African Sub-Regions. A Report of the Fourteenth Ordinary Sessions of the Member Head of States.* Retrieved on March 3, 2000 from Htpp://www.theperspective.org.

Economic Watch (2012). *Ethnic Tension in Liberia and identity Crisis.* London, United Kingdom: I.B. Publishers.

Furley, O. (1995). *Conflict in Africa.* London, United Kingdom: I.B. Publishers.

Hlophe, S.S. (19179). *Class, Ethnicity and Politics in Liberia: The Tubman and Tolbert Administration; 1944- 1980.* Washington Dc: American University Press.

Huband, M. (1998). *The Liberian Civil War.* London, United Kingdom: Frank Class Publishers.

Jah, A.O. (2000). *Conflict Resolutions in Africa: A Case Study of the Organization of African Unity's (OAU) Peacekeeping Force in Chard from*

1981-1982. An Unpublished Doctoral Dissertations, University of Wisconsin.

Lawyers Committee for Human Rights (1986). *Liberia: A Promise Betrayed-Report on Human Rights in Liberia*. New York, New York: Lawyers Committee for Human Rights Press Section.

Liebenow, J. G. (1987). *Liberia: The Quest for Democracy*. Bloomington, Indiana: Indiana University Press.

Marinelli, L. A. (1964). The New Liberia: A Historical and Political Survey. New York, New York: Paegar.

Milligan, R.T. (1989). Bolahun: Liberia West Africa. New York, New York: Vantage.

Mitchell, C. (1996). *Ethnic Conflict and International Interventions in Liberia*. Princeton, New Jersey: Princeton University Press.

Moniba, H.F. (1992). *The Liberian Politics Today: Some Personal Observations*. Monrovia, Liberia: Sabonah.

Mutua, M. W. (2008). *Kenya's Quest for Democracy: Challenges and Changes in African Politics*. Buffalo, New York: Rienner Publishers.

Nelson, H. (1984). Liberia: A Country Study Foreign Area Studies. Washington DC US Government Printing Office.

Olson, D. (1996). History and Hope: Liberia's Battle. Christian Century. 2(3) 924.

Richardson, N. R. (1959). *Liberia Past and Present*. London, United Kingdom: Diplomatic Press.

Sawyer. A. C. (1992). *The Emergence of Autocracy in Liberia: A Tragedy and Challenge*. San Francisco, California: Institute for Contemporary Studies (ISC) Center for Self Governance.

Sawyer, A.C. (1987). *Effective Immediately, Dictatorship in Liberia. 1980–1986.* San Francisco, California: Institute for Contemporary Studies (ISC) Center for Self-Governance.

Sirleaf, A.M. (2000). *The Rolle of the Economic Community of West African States (ECOWAS) in the Liberia Civil Conflict, 1990-1997: Case Study of Conflict Management.* Washington, DC: Blackology Research Development Institute.

Tesler, M.A. (1983). *Liberia's Difficult March Toward Civilian Rule.* Hanover, New Hampshire: New Hampshire University.

Williams, G.I.H. (2002). *Liberia, The Heart of Darkness: Accounts of Liberia's Civil War and its Destabilizing Effects in West Africa.* Victoria, Canada: Trafford Publishing.

www.ingramcontent.com/pod-product-compliance
Lightning Source LLC
Chambersburg PA
CBHW030522290526
45786CB00004B/1572